THE SECONDHAND SNEAKERS

Jan Burchett and Sara Vogler
Illustrated by S. G. Brooks

Rigby®

A Harcourt Achieve Imprint

www.Rigby.com
1-800-531-5015

Hannah was eight years old and the youngest in her family. She had three older brothers, two older sisters, four older boy cousins, and three older girl cousins. Hannah loved being part of such a big family because there were always enough people for a picnic, a party, or a baseball game.

But there was one thing that Hannah hated. Everyone passed on their old clothes to her, and that meant she had a lot of secondhand clothes!

"Hannah really loves secondhand clothes!" said her family, completely misunderstanding.

One morning Hannah discovered that her toe was peeking right through her sneakers. She was delighted because they were horrible, smelly old sneakers that had come from her cousin Sarah.

Then she had an awful, sinking feeling that Mom would be sure to find her another secondhand pair. So Hannah decided not to tell her.

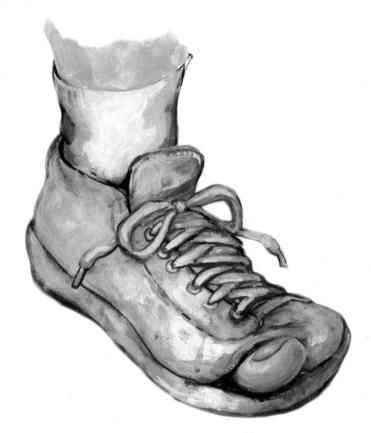

But eagle-eyed Mom saw Hannah's toe peeking through the hole. "I'll have to get you another pair, Hannah," said Mom.

Hannah's awful, sinking feeling went away because she thought Mom might buy her some new sneakers!

Hannah ran to get her coat to go shopping, but Mom went to the closet and began to dig through things.

Hannah's awful, sinking feeling came back.

"You can have Jennifer's old sneakers," Mom called cheerfully from the closet. "I know they're in this cave somewhere!"

Hannah remembered her sister's bright green sneakers with the bells on them that jingled when she walked. Everyone heard her coming!

At last Mom came out frowning and said, "I can't find them."

"Good," Hannah whispered.

"Come on," called Mom. "We're going to go out."

"Hooray," thought Hannah, "Mom's taking me shopping after all!"

However, when they got to the main street, Mom walked past all the stores and didn't stop until they came to Aunt Rita's house.

"Hannah needs some sneakers," she told Aunt Rita.

"Well, you've come to the right place," joked Aunt Rita, "because I've got just the thing!"

"Oh no! Secondhand sneakers again!" thought Hannah.

Aunt Rita reached up to the highest shelf and opened a lot of boxes, but she only found a yo-yo, some toy cars, and a ski glove with a missing thumb.

Hannah's hopes began to rise again.

"Wait a minute," said Aunt Rita, reaching to the back of the shelf and pulling out a backpack.

She passed the backpack to Hannah, and there inside, nested in old yellowing newspaper, was a pair of sneakers.

The sneakers looked like they had been hiding on the top shelf for years. They were brown, ugly, and very old-fashioned.

"They belonged to your cousin Marvin, and they were his favorites," explained Aunt Rita.

Hannah dragged along behind Mom all the way home, wearing Marvin's horrible old sneakers and feeling really silly.

"Why would my family put me through this?" she thought to herself.

And then Hannah, who was usually helpful, decided she would teach her family a lesson. She would no longer do anything to help them.

The next day, Hannah put on Marvin's old sneakers. She didn't want to, but she had no choice. It was either wear the sneakers or go barefoot!

"Hannah," said Mom, "Mrs. Esposito needs to borrow a few eggs. Can you take these to her?"

As Mom handed Hannah the egg carton, Hannah opened her mouth to say "No!" but then she felt a strange feeling in her feet. Before she knew what was happening, the sneakers started walking!

The sneakers walked Hannah and the eggs out of the house, down the block, and right to Mrs. Esposito's door. Mrs. Esposito thanked Hannah, and the shoes marched her right back home.

When Hannah got home, Mom was very pleased with her and exclaimed, "Wow, that was quick!"

"It wasn't me—it was the sneakers," said Hannah.

"I'm so glad you like them," said Mom happily.

The next day, it was Hannah's turn to walk Monty, the family dog.

As Monty ran up to her with his leash in his mouth, Hannah announced, "I'm not taking you anywhere because I'm not going to be helpful today."

Monty sat and begged, but Hannah folded her arms and did not look at him.

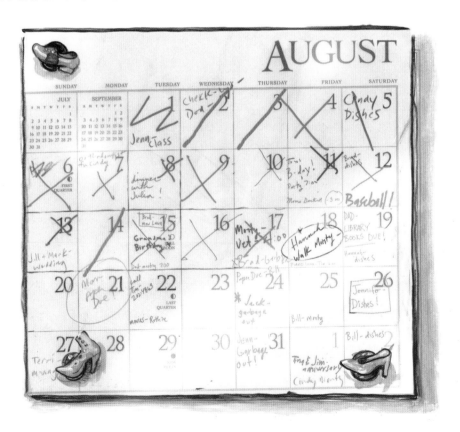

Then she felt the strange feeling in her feet, and, before she knew it, her sneakers took her to the kitchen door, pushed it open, and marched her out, with Monty following closely behind still holding his leash. The sneakers walked Hannah up the street, through the park, and around the lake twice, while Monty followed along happily at her side.

Hannah and Monty fell in a hot, tired heap when they got home.

"Thanks for walking Monty without being reminded!" said Dad.

"It wasn't me," said Hannah. "It was the sneakers."

"I'm so glad you like them," said Dad happily.

The next day was Saturday, and when
Hannah got up, her mind was buzzing
with a smart idea. She put on her socks,
but stuffed the sneakers under her bed.

"Now I can't be helpful," she said
to herself, grinning, "because I've lost
my sneakers!"

She skipped down to breakfast.

"Can someone take my books back to the library for me?" said Dad, dealing out waffles. "I have to take the boys to their baseball game."

"Sorry, Dad," said Jennifer, "but Katie and I are going fishing with Granddad."

"And I have to get my report done for work on Monday," said Mom.

"Can you go, Hannah?" asked Dad.

"I'd love to," said Hannah sweetly, "but I can't find my sneakers anywhere and I can't go out barefoot."

"But your sneakers are right behind you!" said Mom.

Hannah turned and jumped. There were her sneakers. They had sneaked up on her!

"I'm glad they weren't lost because I know you really like your sneakers," said Dad.

Before she could stop herself, Hannah had stepped into her sneakers, and the laces had tied themselves up.

Hannah felt the strange feeling in her feet once again, and the sneakers marched her around the table. Dad handed her the books, and the sneakers took her out the front door.

Hannah tried with all her might to stop her shoes from taking her to the library. She tried to sit down, but the sneakers kept on walking. She tried to grab ahold of a mailbox, but the sneakers kept on walking. She tried to take the sneakers off, but the laces had tied themselves into tight knots.

The sneakers marched her right into the library where Hannah turned Dad's books in.

Hannah was fed up with her horrible, helpful sneakers. She wanted to have some fun, so she decided to go to the park and just hoped that her secondhand sneakers wouldn't mind.

Hannah skipped along the sidewalk, and the sneakers skipped along, too. She marched like a soldier, and so did the sneakers.

"At last," she said, "I'm in charge!"

Hannah had just started to head toward the swings when she saw Mrs. Kelly, a young mother who lived on her street. Mrs. Kelly was coming home from the grocery store, pushing her twins in their stroller. Her grocery bag had broken, the groceries were all over the sidewalk, and the babies were crying!

Hannah felt that strange feeling in her feet, and she just knew that the sneakers were going to make her help Mrs. Kelly.

"Oh, no you don't," she said firmly. "I want to go on the swings."

But of course the sneakers marched her over to Mrs. Kelly instead, and Hannah just couldn't stop them.

"Can I help?" she said uneasily.

Hannah picked up the groceries, trying to balance them all in her arms. Then she gave the twins a big smile and made them laugh.

"Thank you, Hannah," said Mrs. Kelly. "You're so helpful."

Hannah checked her watch. There was still time for her to go back to the swings, but she saw that Mrs. Kelly seemed very tired and didn't have any way to carry all of her groceries home.

"I'll carry your groceries home for you," Hannah said.

When they got to Mrs. Kelly's house, Hannah helped Mrs. Kelly put all the groceries away. Then she played with the twins until it was time for their naps. It was too late now to go back to the park, but she didn't mind.

"You are a very kind girl," said Mrs. Kelly, waving good-bye to Hannah.

"I enjoyed myself," said Hannah as she realized that she actually *did* have fun. She remembered that she really did like helping people—and without the sneakers telling her to!

That night Hannah was clearing the dishes away when the phone rang. Her mom answered it, and when she hung up, she gave Hannah a big, unexpected hug.

"That was Mrs. Kelly," she said, "and she was telling me how you came to help her. I am so proud of you."

"You have been so helpful these past few days that Dad and I think you deserve a treat," said Mom. "So tomorrow I'm taking you to the mall to buy something just for you. What would you like?"

Hannah didn't wait to be asked twice—
"A brand-new pair of sneakers, please!"
she answered.